arts of
clay

arts

# of clay

by christine price

CHARLES SCRIBNER'S SONS
NEW YORK

Library of Congress Cataloging in Publication Data
Price, Christine, 1928-
    Arts of clay.
    SUMMARY: An illustrated survey of clay artwork made
by various cultures.
    1. Pottery, Primitive—History
2. Pottery—History
[1. Pottery—History]   I. Title
NK3795.P74   738.3'83   77-23103
ISBN 0-684-15120-0

Illustration on page 1:
ANCIENT POT
Panama

Page 2: WATER POT
Jos, Nigeria

Page 6: TURTLE-SHAPED
VESSEL Fiji

Page 7: WATER POT, Zaire

4

the pots in this book are a

mixture of old and new. Some of them were made by Indian potters of the Americas long before the white men arrived as discoverers of a New World. Other pots are older still, made in Europe and Asia in prehistoric times.

Dates for the ancient pots can be found in the list of illustrations at the end of the book. Dates and places of making are important to know. Forms and styles of pottery change through the centuries, and different peoples have created different kinds of pots.

Yet when we look at old pots side by side with new ones, distances of time and space seem to melt away. The village potters of today and those of the ancient past all belong to one world. To these potters of past and present, creators of the arts of clay, this book is dedicated.

BLACK POTTERY PIPE BOWL
Cameroon
(*See page 48*)

contents

arts of clay

8

the potter's workplace is a

cave, a long ledge on the mountainside, sheltered by a great rocky overhang. The morning sunshine blazes on the steep slope of the mountain, but under the cave roof, darkened by the smoke of many fires, the air is cool. The potter stands barefooted on the sandy floor and stoops down to build her pot with thick brown coils of clay laid on a flat slab of rock. The light gleams on the thin hoop earrings that swing from her ears and the wide collar of blue beads about her neck.

She is making the top half of a large water jar. The pot gradually grows taller as she adds more coils to the first ring of clay on the rock. She smooths the walls of the pot and pulls them up, walking around her work, bent double. Her long, dark-skinned hands move gracefully inside and outside the growing shape. Her only tools are a narrow strip of wood and an oval

Opposite:
WATER POT
Kenya,
Pokot people

9

piece cut from the hard, dry skin of a calabash. Water to wet her fingers is close at hand, held in the bottom of a broken pot.

The potter is a woman of the Pokot people, farmers in East Africa. Her cave on the hillside overlooks the hazy distance of the Kerio Valley, where her people have their fields, and away to the north stretches the range of mountains that leads up to their sacred peak, Mtelo.

From the mouth of the cave she can look straight down on the round thatched roofs and neat court-yards of her neighbors' houses, dotted about over the hillside and linked by winding paths. In the still morning air the voices of women and children far below rise sharp and clear. At the foot of the hill an earth road runs past the *kokwa* tree, the tree of meetings. Beyond the road lie the valley fields, made green and rich by the water led down through long channels from springs in the hills. The maize stands tall. The banana plants are heavy with fruit. Only the fallow land, cut off from the life-giving water, looks dry and brown.

The potter's people are rooted in their land. All their lives they work with the earth and the water that makes it fruitful. The potter too works with earth and water. Her pots are built of damp clay, dug from the earth; and they will hold food from the fields and water from the mountain springs. She works to fill her people's needs, and their needs and her way of working are as ancient as the art of pottery

Farming and making pots go hand in hand. The first potters, in most parts of the world, were also the first farmers. They had given up the wandering life of Stone Age hunters to settle down in villages and grow their food. Long before pots were made, people had discovered that clay could be shaped with the fingers, then baked in a fire to make it strong and hard. They modeled the clay into little figures of humans and animals. Some of these were probably children's toys, like the small clay cattle that are made today by young boys of the Pokot.

In the Middle East, nine thousand years ago, clay was also used in building weatherproof houses and making hearths and ovens for cooking. When the farmers' harvests were good, the grain was stored in dry, clay-lined pits or in large clay vessels built into the walls of the houses. Out of these many uses of clay came the idea of making pots.

Opposite: WATER POT
Right: TOY BULL MADE
OF UNBAKED CLAY
Both from Kenya, Pokot people

11

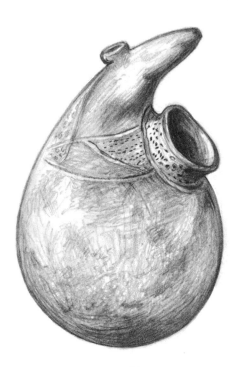

In the New World, the first Indian potters lived on the northwest coast of South America. They were fisherfolk rather than farmers, and the wares they made, about five thousand years ago, look strangely like the pottery of ancient Japan.

The potter's art was born at different times in different places, but almost everywhere it was an art of women. Farmers' wives made their own clay vessels for holding food and water and fired them in their own cooking fires. The familiar forms of woven baskets, hollow gourds, or fat leather waterbags served as models for some of the earliest pots. The potters shaped the clay with their hands and with a few simple tools—pieces of wood and dry calabash, an old corncob, or a smooth, water-worn stone.

The women's ways of building pots, passed down in families from mother to daughter, changed little through the centuries, even after the invention of the potter's wheel. Wheel-thrown pottery, up until recent

Left: GOURD-SHAPED VESSEL
Kenya, Pokot people
Opposite: FESTIVE DRINKING VESSEL
Colombia, Guahibo people

times, was always the work of men. They were pro-
fessional craftsmen, making their living by their craft.
As the wheel spun around, many pots of the same size
and shape could be turned out at high speed.

Wheel-thrown pottery was made in the Middle
East and in China about 3000 B.C. Potters took up
the new technique in Japan and throughout Asia,
around the Mediterranean, and in northern Europe.
They built closed kilns for firing big batches of pots
at much higher temperatures than in the old open
fires. Finer and harder kinds of clay could be fired,
and pots were made beautiful with glazes of glowing
color. Potters were no longer limited to a few earth
colors for painting their wares. All the colors of the
rainbow were at their command, and the shape of the
clay pot was often less important than its marvelous
skin of decoration. Exquisite pieces of pottery, made
to adorn the palaces of kings, were gazed upon as
works of art. Pots had come a long way from their
origins as simple things molded from earth and water.

Yet some of the finest pottery in the world has been
made without the wheel. In the lands of black Africa,
in North and South America, and on islands of the
South Pacific all pottery was built by hand. The potter's wheel was unknown until it was brought in by
outsiders, and the art of glazing was unexplored. Pots
might be richly decorated with painting, especially
in the Americas, but often the plain color of the fired

clay is the color of the pot. The texture of the clay—smooth and polished, or rough and gritty—invites touching, feeling, and handling. Our hands respond to these things that other hands have made.

Pottery is, above all, a work of the hand. The clay has been shaped, not by hard chiseling, grinding, or cutting, but by the strong, rhythmic movements of the potter's hands. Even when pottery is made without the wheel, it tends to be round in form. The curve and the circle are more natural shapes for people to make in their movements than the square or the straight line. Footprints in sand or snow make patterns of curves. Dancers move in curves, and many dances have the form of a circle.

When the Pokot potter stoops low and walks around her work, the turning of her whole body is shaping the clay. After her newly made pot has hardened in the fire, its form will always show the pattern and rhythm of her way of working.

Pottery, molded of earth and water, must be finished in fire. The soft clay, after firing, is not only hard but almost everlasting. A pot is easily smashed, but the pieces will endure. Fragments of pottery are often the principal relics left behind by peoples of ancient times. When broken pots made hundreds of years ago can be fitted together again, they stand before us as though they were finished yesterday, still bearing the marks of the potter's hand.

Earth, fire, and water and the skill of the hand—these are the makings of the pottery we shall see in this book. These pots, some new, some very old, were built without the wheel, and no paint or glaze was used to decorate the clay. Some of the pottery was made for sacred ceremonies or for burial with the dead, but much of it was to fill the common needs of daily life. We shall begin by looking at the humblest pots of all, designed for hard use and never considered to be works of art—the pots for cooking.

COOKING POTS
Left: **Nigeria, Ibo people**
Right: **American Indian, Papago**

15

pots for cooking must be strong

and sturdy, their shapes adapted to their use, but there is still some room for decoration.

The Navajo Indian woman who made the large pot opposite put two bands of molded clay around the top, according to the custom of her people. The Navajo call these clay necklaces the "beads of the pot."

The open fire in which this pot was baked has left the brown clay blotched with a big firemarks of black and gray. While the vessel was still red-hot from the coals, the potter smeared it, inside and out, with resin of the piñon pine. The newly fired clay, like all plain earthenware, is porous and soaks up liquids. The resin helps to seal it.

Some Navajo potters mix their clay with ground-up fragments of ancient pottery from the ruins of old Indian pueblos. This makes the clay easier to work with and less likely to crack in the firing. The old pottery gives life to the new.

COOKING POTS
Right: **Navajo**
Opposite: **Pokot**

17

Most clay cooking pots, especially old ones, have rounded bottoms instead of a flat base to stand on. How the rest of the vessel is shaped and decorated depends on the forms the potter has learned to make and the types of pots her people need for cooking different foods.

This vessel from ancient Britain, thick and heavy, is covered with small patterns pressed into the damp clay. The West African pot is casserole-shaped, its smooth body decorated with elegant geometric designs in low relief, while the old Indian bowl from

COOKING POTS
Left: **Prehistoric Britain**
Opposite above: **Nigeria**
Below: **Ancient Mexico**

Mexico has been made rough and lumpy, harsh to the touch. Indian pots as rough outside as this one were often polished inside with a stone before firing, to make the clay less porous and easier to clean. The potters of Casas Grandes, where this bowl comes from, also made fine black pottery, polished inside and out.

Pots for cooking beans have always been important in the Americas. Beans were a staple food of the Indians even before the cultivation of corn, and long before the first Indian pottery was made.

Among the Pueblo Indian people of the Southwest, the small pueblo of Picuris is famous for making bean pots. Plain and simple in shape, their only decorations are the sparkling flecks of mica in the pale, desert-brown clay and the dark, smoky marks left by the firing. Indians and white people alike say that beans are best cooked in a Picuris pot.

The potters of Fiji in the South Pacific make cooking wares as plain and practical as those of Picuris.

Above:
ANCIENT BEAN POT
Mexico, Maya people

Left:
MODERN BEAN POT
Picuris, New Mexico

20

But their way of working is not the way of the Pueblo Indians. A Fiji pot grows to the sound of a steady, swift tap-tapping. The potter is beating the outside with a wooden paddle. Inside, against the wall of the pot, she holds a smooth, rounded stone. Pressed between the stone and the tapping paddle, the clay wall is gradually squeezed upward to the height the potter wants.

COOKING POTS
Left: **Kenya**
Pokot people
Right: **Fiji**

Like the Navajo, the Fijian women paint their pottery with resin after firing, but only to make it bright and shiny for sale to strangers. A pot for home use is left plain. Fiji cooking vessels, often huge in size, are propped over the fire in a tilted position, resting on three stones or clay supports. This makes it easier to reach down inside the pot for the steaming *dalo* roots or whatever is cooking.

The Indian "shoe-pot," with its mouth off-center, could be laid on its side on the fire without spilling. This odd-shaped form was popular in Central America, and sometimes an Indian potter would make a shoe-pot with an animal head and a set of stumpy legs.

Legs on a cooking pot can be very useful. Potters

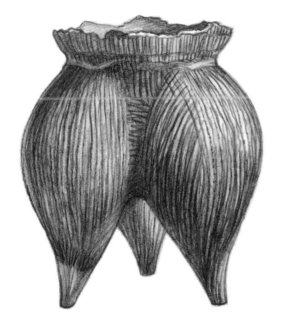

of ancient China discovered this and made three-legged pots that stood firmly over the fire.

Some of the early Chinese potters worked with the "paddle and anvil" method used by Fijians today. The anvil was a mushroom-shaped piece of pottery instead of a stone, and the paddle was wrapped with cords that printed their pattern on the clay. The three-legged pot above was meant to stand in the smoke of cooking fires, but the idea of putting legs on a pot led to the making of vessels that had no place in the kitchen. Some of these were pots for pouring, fit to serve wine at a feast.

Left: TRIPOD POT
Ancient China
Right: SHOE-POT
WITH LEGS
Ancient Mexico

23

pots for pouring should have a

spout that pours without dripping. Otherwise their design can be as simple or elaborate as the potter wants to make it.

At first sight, these lovely vessels from ancient Iran look more like sculptured animals than pots. Yet anyone trying to copy their forms in clay will find it quite

impossible to do so if he thinks of them simply as figures of magnificent humpbacked bulls.

First and foremost, they are spouted pots for pouring. The hollow body of the animal is a vessel lying on its side, rather like an Indian shoe-pot, supported on four short legs. The spout at one end develops into the animal's head, adorned with splendid horns.

These bulls are domestic cattle, not the wild ones that were hunted by prehistoric men and portrayed in wonderful paintings on the walls of caves. Among the early cattle-herding peoples, bulls were revered for their strength and courage. They were even worshiped as gods.

BULL-SHAPED WATER VESSELS Ancient Iran

25

Pouring vessels in the form of beasts and birds, real or fantastic, were popular in the Middle East in ancient times. This bird-shaped pot, like the two bulls, comes from northern Iran. The bird is made of red pottery, smoothly polished, and its wide-eyed human face is topped by a royal crown. Such fancy vessels were made for palaces and temples, but even simple village pots, old and new, carry on the tradition of animal design.

The water jug opposite, from a farmhouse in Honduras, has a little bull's head for a spout. The shape

Right: **WATER POT**
Java, Indonesia
Left: **BIRD-SHAPED VESSEL**
Ancient Iran

26

of this modern pot probably goes back to ancient Indian forms, but the bull's head owes its origin to the Spaniards. The Spanish conquerors brought the

Left:
FARMHOUSE WATER POT
Honduras
Right:
OLD INDIAN POT
Santa Marta, Colombia

27

28

first cattle to America, and some of the Indians revered the bull, as people had done in the Old World for centuries.

A human head, beautifully modeled, crowns this "royal jug" from Africa, a vessel fit for a king's palace. The head alone seems mysteriously to change the whole pot into a human form.

The idea of making clay vessels in human shape is very old. Little models of people were among the earliest arts of clay, and to this day, the parts of a clay pot are named after the parts of the human person— body and shoulder, neck, mouth and lip.

The simple jar above, made by a potter of prehistoric Europe, shows how a pot with two projecting spouts can be transformed into a human figure with upraised arms.

Opposite:
ROYAL JUG, Zaire
Above:
POT IN HUMAN FORM
Ancient Czechoslovakia

29

ANCIENT MEXICAN POTS
Left: **Teotihuacán**
Right: **Oaxaca**
Opposite: **Michoacán**

A Mexican potter, also making a twin-spouted jar, added a human head, hands, and feet, modeled on the body of the pot.

Pouring pots with two spouts took many forms in the Americas. One of the best known is the graceful "wedding jar" of the Pueblo Indians. The jar opposite was made by a potter of Santa Clara pueblo in New Mexico. She built it with coils of clay, smoothed and polished. The pot was fired in an outdoor fire, covered over with dry sheep dung to hold in the smoke. This way of firing gave the finished jar its gleaming blackness, a mark of the famous Santa Clara pottery.

30

Black pots are considered beautiful in many parts of the world. Potters of Cameroon in West Africa blacken their wares by rubbing them with the juice of palm leaves before firing. Among the pots they make are small bowls to hold rich yellow palm oil, an important food of the people. In the past, these bowls were pots for pouring, with a short spout opposite the

Right: WEDDING JAR
Santa Clara, New Mexico

upstanding handle, but the bowl we see here has in place of the spout a little pointed nubbin of clay. The six legs the bowl stands on are in a springy, bent-kneed position, like the legs of African dancers. The Mexican bowl opposite stands on three straight legs, firmly rooted on the ground. The African bowl seems about to jump up and dance!

bowls and cups are usually simpler in form than spouted pots, more varied in design than pots for cooking. The Mexican bowl below is a sauce boat and also a mortar for grinding food. The raised pattern inside was made by pressing the wet clay over a mold. Bowls like this one, a standard design of the potters of Acatlán, are about as simple in shape as a bowl can be, but the addition of legs gives any pot a special character, as we have seen.

GRAVY BOAT
Acatlán, Mexico

ANCIENT BOWLS
WITH LEGS
Right: **Hasanlu, Iran**
Below: **Monte Alban,**
Oaxaca, Mexico

The three splayed-out legs of this small gray cup from ancient Iran seem to balance the extraordinary animal handle on the top. The shape of the cup itself is similar to the African oil bowl on page 32, but, unlike the bowl, the little cup was not meant to be used by living people. It was an offering in a tomb.

34

Making bowls with legs was a common practice in ancient America. Often the legs were rounded and hollow, like those on the little vessel below, made in Nicaragua about seven hundred years ago. On many bowls, though not on this one, the hollow legs had pebbles of clay sealed inside them. Then the pot became a rattle, a popular musical instrument.

The legs of Indian bowls could also be in the form of human beings or other living creatures. They could

ANCIENT BOWLS WITH LEGS
Top left and right: **Panama**
Left: **Nicaragua**

35

ANCIENT AMERICAN BOWLS
Left: **Ecuador**
Right: **Costa Rica**

be immensely long and lavishly decorated, or as simple as the four legs of this bowl from Ecuador, which rise like growing things from a round base.

The two bowls opposite, also with four legs, are the work of Indian potters of North America. They come from the southeastern woodlands, where the Indians made a variety of fine pottery before the invasion of the white men. The animal-shaped bowl, with its catlike head and stumpy tail, represents a panther, a favorite subject of these potters.

The bowl at the right includes four rattles, not in its legs but inside the hollow pointed projections that give the bowl its four-cornered form. The scroll patterns decorating these pots were not only popular

ANCIENT AMERICAN BOWLS
Arkansas

with the Indians. Pottery patterned with scrolls and spirals was also made in Africa, the South Pacific, and ancient Europe. On the prehistoric Romanian bowl below, the twin spirals almost suggest a pair of eyes.

Bowls, like spouted vessels, could take a human form. The Danish "face-pot" opposite, made nearly five thousand years ago, has two eyes scratched in the clay. Eyes were a symbol of the Mother Goddess, worshiped by many peoples of Europe in Neolithic

BOWLS WITH MOLDED SPIRAL DECORATION
Left: **Papua New Guinea**
Center: **Nigeria**
Right: **Ancient Romania**

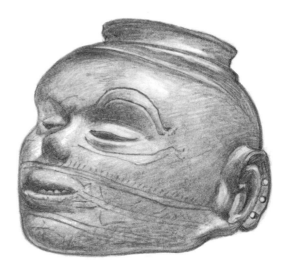

times. Peering out from under modeled brows, the
eyes give this simple bowl the look of a human head.
The Indian bowl at the right has actually been shaped
as a head, perhaps the head of an enemy killed in
battle.

These two pots were buried in tombs. Both the
Indians and the tribal folk of ancient Europe had a
deep belief in life after death and furnished the
tombs of important people with weapons, ornaments,
and pottery.

Left: FACE-POT
Ancient Denmark
Right: INDIAN HEAD-POT
Arkansas

39

Besides making bowls in the shape of heads or complete human figures, Indian potters would sometimes model a figure on the outside of a bowl.

The large pot opposite shows an African version of the same idea. This vessel from Nigeria was used in the worship of the Yam Spirit, who blessed the farmers' fields with heavy crops. Instead of one figure, the African potter has made a whole row of them, rich in detail and lively enough to leap off the pot.

The seated man modeled on the Indian bowl seems calm and still, and the whole vessel is simple in outline. Yet no one knew better than the Indian artists how to make clay come to life.

ANCIENT MEXICAN
BOWL Oaxaca

Above: ANCIENT
MEXICAN BOWL
Teotihuacán
Right: CEREMONIAL
BOWL **Nigeria,
Ibo people**

41

THE OLD FIRE GOD
Ancient Mexico,
Maya people

This masterwork of a potter of Mexico is a bowl for sacred offerings, held by a figure of the Fire God. The gaunt old god, wrinkled and gap-toothed, is seated in a conch shell that curves up over his head.

The mournful hoot of the conch-shell trumpet was a familiar sound in ancient Mexico, and this pottery conch is made to be blown like a trumpet. The hollow figure of the god is a whistle, and the round legs of the bowl are rattles. The vessel is filled with music!

The old God of Fire, modeled so vividly here, was one of the most ancient gods of Mexico, and he was worshiped in North America too. Among the Algonkian Indians, Our Grandfather Fire was the kindly god of the family hearth. The smoke rising through the smokehole carried his messages to the Great Spirit.

For people the world over, fire is a holy thing, mysterious and wonderful, whether it is the hearth fire, the flame of lamps at night, or the smoke of incense. But fire is also terrible, a mighty destroyer, to be feared, respected, and controlled.

Pottery vessels, hardened in fire, can endure the heat of the flames. And so, from the early days of pottery, there have been pots to hold fire.

INCENSE BURNER
Ancient Mexico,
Mixtec people

43

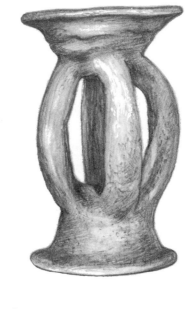

pots to hold fire include plain every-
day wares for all the home uses of fire—lamps and candlesticks, chafing dishes and stoves.

The clay lamp above, from Ghana in West Africa, was made by a potter of the Ashanti people. Although its shape follows an old Ashanti pattern, the lamp looks a little like the four-legged bowl from Ecuador on page 36. That bowl may also have been a pot to hold fire, a chafing dish with a small flame burning in the base to warm food in the bowl.

The large pot opposite, also from West Africa, is a cooking stove. The design of its graceful clover-leaf

44

opening is strictly practical. A round-bottomed cooking pot will sit firmly on the three projecting points. Stoves like this one are sold in the open-air pottery market of the town of Gao in Mali, on the great River Niger. They are traveling stoves, used for cooking the meals of the boatmen aboard the long canoes that journey up and down the river.

COOKING STOVE
Gao, Mali

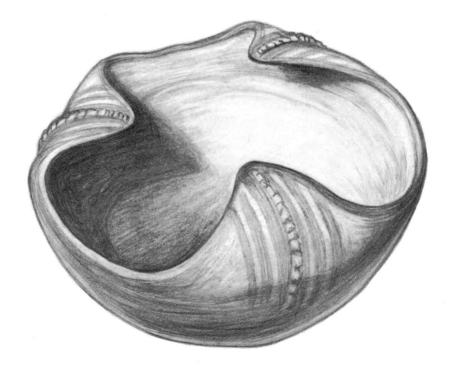

INDIAN PIPE BOWLS
FROM THE SOUTHEAST
Above: **Alabama**
Below: **Kentucky**

Pots to hold fire at religious ceremonies are more elaborate than those for domestic use. The incense burner shown on page 43 is one of many beautiful vessels made in ancient Mexico for burning *copal* incense as an offering to the gods.

In North America, the Indians had no copal to burn for a sweet-smelling smoke. Their incense was tobacco.

To the Indians tobacco was a sacred plant, a gift from the Creator. Smoking was not a pastime but a holy act. In woodland and prairie, mountain and desert, smoking was a vital part of Indian rituals and solemn gatherings. From Mexico down into northern South America the Indians mostly smoked tobacco in cigars. Pipes were used for smoking in parts of Mexico and in the far south of the continent; and almost everywhere in North America, except among Pueblo peoples of the Southwest, pipe smoking was the rule. The sharing of a pipe of tobacco welcomed guests, strengthened friendships, and made peace between enemies. Many of these pipes were modeled of clay. They were miniature pots to sold a sacred fire.

Some of the finest of them, made by the Indians of the Southeast and the Iroquois to the north, were in the form of animals or people. The Iroquois bear's-head pipe even has a tiny rattle in the head. The pipe bowls opposite, from Kentucky and Alabama, would have been fitted with long stems for smoking the strong southern tobacco. When a pipe was passed around in a gathering of men, each would send out six puffs of smoke—to the four directions, to the sky, and to the earth.

White men invading the Americas learned from the Indians how to smoke and carried tobacco throughout the world. The pipe bowl below, worn smooth with long use, was made in West Africa, where tobacco from America was introduced by slave traders.

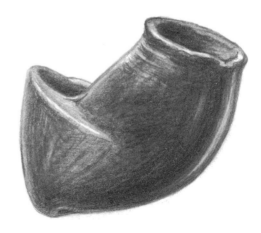

47

**BLACK POTTERY PIPE
BOWL WITH WOODEN STEM
Cameroon**
(*See page 5 for front view*)

African peoples were accustomed to using other
plants for smoking. They readily accepted the American tobacco and soon began to grow it for themselves.
Tobacco smoking was a pleasure and to smoke a hand-
some pipe was a sign of high standing. In western
Cameroon, where this long-stemmed pipe was made,
every important man has his drinking horn for palm
wine and his pipe for tobacco.

Clay pipes in Africa, traditionally the work of men,

48

are made in many different shapes. The pipe like a tiny vase of smooth red pottery comes from Mali. The Zambian pipe at the left has a wide bowl supported by a little sculptured antelope.

These miniature pots to hold fire will fit in the hollow of the hand. Pots to hold water are sometimes too mighty to lift. Fire is warmth and light and the smoke of offerings; water is the sacred source of life. Vessels to carry water and to keep it cool and sweet go back to the beginnings of pottery, for without water the people would die.

AFRICAN PIPE BOWLS
Left: **Zambia**
Right: **Mali**

50

pots to hold water are made in

ample rounded forms. Some of the loveliest are the work of peoples living in hot and thirsty lands, where the sun's fire scorches the earth and the people must pray to the gods for rain. There the first potters learned that fire-hardened clay would hold not only the heat of fire but the coolness of water. A big clay pot is a natural water cooler, kept always cold by the water seeping slowly through its porous walls.

Even in rich green countries of swamp and tropical forest, people worship the gods of water, and everywhere the work of fetching water from rivers, springs, and village wells is a daily task that never ends. Before the making of pottery, people carried water in leather bags and the hollow shells of gourds and coconuts, as they still do in some parts of the world.

Above: LID OF A VESSEL
USED IN THE WORSHIP OF
A WATER GOD
Nigeria, Yoruba people
Opposite: LARGE VESSEL
FOR STORING WATER **Mali**

GOURD-SHAPED POTS
Two above: **Malaysia**
Right: **American Indian,
Apache**
Below: **Ancient America,
Arkansas**

The shapes of those early water vessels were copied by the first potters. The gourd was the favorite form. A bottle-shaped pot with a round body and narrow neck will hold water without spilling and will not crack as easily in the drying and firing as a shallow, wide-mouthed vessel.

52

Potters in Asia, Africa, and the Americas took the gourd as their model. Some followed its form exactly. Others added a flat base, tripod legs, or a pair of handles and decorated their pots with designs cut into the clay walls or worked in relief.

The potters also saw in the bottle form the beginnings of a human shape; and vessels for water, like

GOURD-SHAPED POTS
Left: **Cameroon**
Center: **Botswana**
Right: **Ancient America, Arkansas**

53

POT WITH HUMAN HEAD
Zaire, Zande people

54

bowls and spouted pots, were turned into images of people. This could be done in many ways—by making the whole vessel into a human figure; by modeling face and arms on the body of the pot; or simply by placing a sculptured head on the long neck of a bottle. For the African artist, the head alone—the most important and powerful part of the body—was enough to create a human image.

**ANCIENT AMERICAN POTS
IN HUMAN SHAPE**
Left: **Panama**
Right: **Colombia**

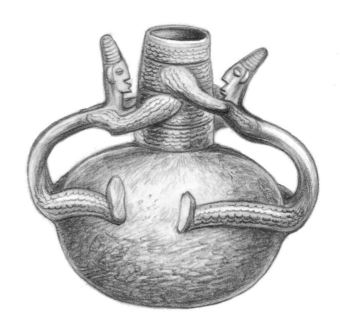

**POT FOR WATER
OR BEER
Zaire, Mangbetu people**

On another African pot lively human figures serve as handles. These are more for decoration than practical use; but the small loop-handles on the two vessels opposite were designed to bear the weight of the water-filled pot. The large, high-necked flask was made in Ecuador about five hundred years ago, in the time of the great empire of the Incas. People traveling the steep paths of the Andes carried vessels like this one on their backs, supported by a tumpline that passed around the forehead or the chest and through the handles of the pot.

The big water jar below is meant to be carried in the same way. This is a modern pot from Ecuador, made by an Indian in a mountain village. With a full

Opposite left:
**OLD WATER POT IN
INCA STYLE**
Right:
**MODERN WATER POT
Both from Ecuador**

56

load of water the vessel would be very heavy, and the potter took great care to make the handles strong. To attach them to the body of the pot, holes were cut in the clay walls and the ends of the handles pushed through and firmly anchored inside and out.

The fingers of the Indian potter, making the handles firm and strong, moved in the same patterns as the skilled hands of the Pokot woman of Africa, at work in her hillside cave. She too is putting handles

on the water vessel she is making. She forms them from two rolls of clay. Then she cuts holes in the walls of the pot, fits in the ends of the handles, and anchors them inside. On the outside, she wraps thin snakes of clay around the handles and smooths them down to strengthen the joining of handle and pot.

Then she draws back to look at her work—the top half of the brown clay vessel, rising from the stone on which she built it. She can do no more today. This morning's work must be left to harden. Then she will turn the vessel upside down and build the lower half of it with rings of clay. She lays aside her tools at the back of the cave where finished pots are drying, waiting to be fired. When the pots are ready, she will gather wood and fire them on a rock ledge close to the cave.

She straightens her back and steps outside into the flaming heat and brightness of the morning. Before her lies the valley, where the earth and water feed the crops and the tall stems of maize reach up toward the sun. She starts down the hillside to her house, walking barefooted along the well-worn path.

A dark, slender woman, proud in her bearing, she is one of the great company of potters everywhere whose hands have made form and loveliness from water, earth, and fire.

LARGE WATER JAR
Mexico

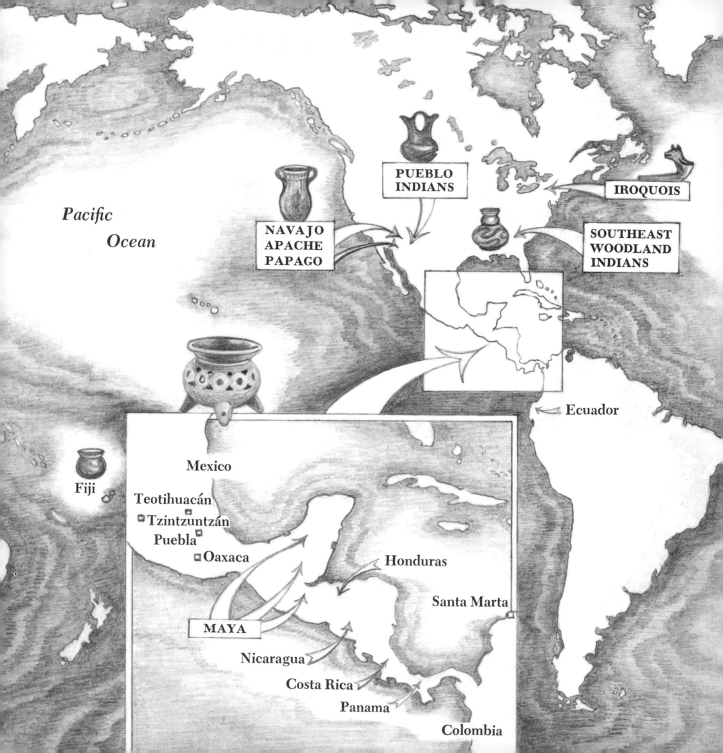

Pacific
Ocean

PUEBLO
INDIANS

IROQUOIS

NAVAJO
APACHE
PAPAGO

SOUTHEAST
WOODLAND
INDIANS

Ecuador

Fiji

Mexico

Teotihuacán
Tzintzuntzán
Puebla
Oaxaca

Honduras

Santa Marta

MAYA

Nicaragua

Costa Rica

Panama

Colombia

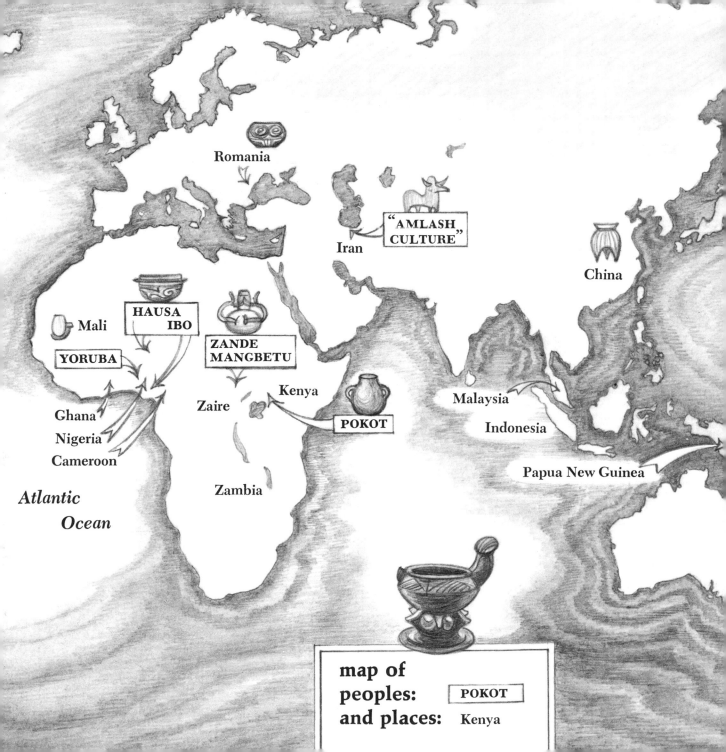

Romania

"AMLASH CULTURE"

Iran

China

Mali

HAUSA IBO

ZANDE MANGBETU

YORUBA

Kenya

Malaysia

Ghana

Zaire

POKOT

Indonesia

Nigeria

Cameroon

Papua New Guinea

Atlantic Ocean

Zambia

map of peoples: POKOT
and places: Kenya

List of Illustrations

The names of some museums and collections are abbreviated as follows: American Museum of Natural History, New York—AMNH; Author's Collection—AC; British Museum, London—BM; Museum of New Mexico, Santa Fe—MNM; Museum of the American Indian, New York—MAI; National Museum of Kenya, Nairobi—NMK; UCLA Museum of Cultural History, Los Angeles—UCLA. (Page numbers appear in **bold** type.)

region, Zaire. MNM. **29** Pot in human shape. Svodín, Slovakia, Czechoslovokia, 4000–3000 B.C. National Museum, Prague. **30** (*left*) Vessel with two spouts. Teotihuacán, Mexico, 250–500 A.D. 7 in. x 6¾ in. MAI. (*right*) Vessel with two spouts and modeled human figure. Monte Alban, Oaxaca, Mexico, 100 B.C.–300 A.D. National Museum of Anthropology, Mexico City. **31** (*left*) Vessel with long spout and additional stirrup-spout in hollow handle. Tzintzuntzán, Michoacán, Mexico, 1250–1500 A.D. 8 in. x 9 in. MAI. (*right*) Polished black wedding jar. Pueblo Indian, Santa Clara, New Mexico, about 1900 A.D. 10 in. x 12¾ in. MAI. **32** Black bowl for palm oil. Bali, Cameroon. 6½ in. x 5¾ in. AC.

bowls and cups

    33 Black-ware gravy boat or food mortar. Acatlán, Mexico. 4½ in. x 6½ in. AC. **34** (*left*) Bowl with three feet shaped like birds' heads. Monte Alban, Oaxaca, Mexico, 1000–1521 A.D. AMNH. (*right*) Three-legged cup. Hasanlu, Azerbaijan, Iran, about 1000 B.C. Archaeology Museum, Teheran. **35** (*left*) Tripod bowl. La Concepción, Chiriquí, Panama, 250–100 B.C. 5½ in. x 10¼ in. MAI. (*center*) Bowl with hollow legs. Granada Mountains, Nicaragua, 1200–1400 A.D. 3 in. x 5 in. AC. (*right*) Bowl with loop-shaped legs. Veraguas, Panama, 1250–1500 A.D. 5½ in. x 10⅜ in. MAI. **36** (*left*) Four-legged bowl. Peripa, Pichincha, Ecuador, 1000–1250 A.D. 6 in. x 6¼ in. MAI. (*right*) Three-legged bowl. Costa Rica, Precolumbian. Collection of Jeannette Mirsky. **37** (*left*) Cat-shaped bowl. Pecan Point, Mississippi County, Arkansas, 1200–1600 A.D. 5 in. x 8 in. MAI. (*right*) Bowl with four hollow projections containing rattles. Greer, Jefferson County, Arkansas, 1250–1500 A.D. 3½ in. x 6¼ in. MAI. **38** (*left*) Bowl with molded spiral decoration accented with paint. Sepik River, Papua New Guinea. Height: 6¾ in. BM. (*center*) Bowl with molded spiral decoration. Nigeria, Ibo people. 10⅛ in. x 16¼ in. Jos Museum, Jos, Nigeria. (*right*) Bowl with molded spiral decoration. Vădastra, Romania, 3500–2700 B.C. Archaeological Institute, Bucharest. **39** (*left*) Bowl with eye motif. Svinø, Denmark. Neolithic. Height: 4¾ in. National Museum, Copenhagen. (*right*) Head-pot. Temple Mound II, Blytheville, Arkansas, 1200–1600 A.D. Height: 6 in. MAI. **40** Bowl in human shape. Monte Negro, Oaxaca, Mexico, 800–600 B.C. National Museum of Anthropology, Mexico City. **41** (*left*) Bowl with seated man. Teotihuacán, Mexico, 400–500 A.D. Height: 4¾ in. National Museum of Anthropology, Mexico City. (*right*) Ceremonial pot for the worship of the Yam Spirit. Osisa, Nigeria, Ibo people, 19th century. Height: 19 in. BM. **42** Bowl with figure of the Fire God. Guaymil, Mexico, Maya people, 900–1200 A.D. 9 in. x 9½ in. MAI. **43** Incense burner. Puebla, Mexico, Mixtec people, 1250–1500 A.D. 3¼ in. x 3¾ in. MAI.

pots to hold fire

    44 (*left*) Lamp with multiple cups. Nigeria, Hausa people (pottery mostly made by men). Height: 15 in. Jos Museum, Jos, Nigeria. (*right*) Lamp. Ghana, Ashanti people. National Museum, Accra, Ghana. **45** Stove; red with black lines painted on the three points that would support a cooking pot. Gao, Mali. 7 in. x 13 in. Collection of Robin and Kendall Mix. **46** (*below*) Gray-ware pipe bowl. American Indian, Kentucky. MAI. (*above*) Gray-ware pipe bowl. American Indian, Alabama. MAI. **47** (*left*) Pipe with bear's head. Iroquois. MAI. (*right*) Black pottery pipe bowl. Mali. 3 in. x 2½ in. AC. **48** Pipe with black pottery bowl and black wooden stem. Bamenda,

Cameroon. Bowl: 4½ in. x 2½ in. Length of stem: 24 in. AC. **49** (*left*) Pipe bowl with animal figure, decorated with red slip. Zambia, Ila or Lozi people. Collection of Jeannette Mirsky. (*right*) Red-ware pipe bowl. Mali. 2⅞ in. x 2⅜ in. AC.

50 Water storage vessel. Mali. UCLA. **51** Lid of vessel used in the worship of Eyinle, a water god. Nigeria, Yoruba people. Height: 10¾ in. BM. **52** (*left*) Two gourd-shaped pots. Perak River, Malaysia. (*center*) Gourd-shaped pot. American Indian, Apache. MNM. (*right*) Three-legged bottle. Van Buren, Crawford County, Arkansas, 1250–1600 A.D. 8½ in. x 5½ in. MAI. **53** (*left*) Black gourd-shaped pot. Cameroon, Bamileke (people). Height: 8 in. BM. (*center*) Milk vessel. Botswana. Height: 10½ in. BM. (*right*) Bottle with incised decoration. Yell County, Arkansas, 1300–1700 A.D. Height: 6½ in. MAI. **54** Vessel with human head. Zaire, Zande people. UCLA. **55** (*left*) Pot in human form. Veraguas, Panama, 1000–1500 A.D. MAI. (*right*) Pot in human form. Santa Marta, Magdalena, Colombia, 1200–1600 A.D. 7½ in. x 8 in. MAI. **56** Pot for water or beer. Zaire, Mangbetu people. AMNH. **57** (*left*) Water pot in *aryballus* shape, typical of Inca pottery. Guachi, Tungurahua, Ecuador, 1450–1525 A.D. 14 in. x 17 in. MAI. (*right*) Water pot (*cántaro*). San Miguel, Ecuador. Diameter: 19 in. From: Gertrude Litto, *South American Folk Pottery*, Watson-Guptill Publications, New York, 1976. **59** Large water jar. Mexico. MNM.